PRAYER NUGGETS

INSPIRING PRAYER JOURNAL

DAILY PRAYER & WISDOM NUGGETS

CAROLINE BIMBO AFOLALU

Copyright © 2022 Caroline Bimbo Afolalu

All rights reserved

No part of this book can be reproduced in any form or by written electronic or mechanical, including photocopying, recording, or by any information retrieval system or otherwise without the prior written permission of the author or publisher.

Published by
Whitstone Books
Croydon UK
May 2022
Printed in Great Britain

Although every precaution has been taken in the preparation of this book, the publisher and author assume no responsibility for errors or omissions. Neither is any liability assumed for damages resulting from the use of the information held herein.

ISBN 978-0-9574755-9-5

THIS JOURNAL BELONGS TO

"Then you will prosper, if you are careful to observe and fulfill the statutes and ordinances which the LORD commanded Moses concerning Israel. Be strong and courageous, do not fear nor be dismayed."

1 CHRONICLES 22:13

CONTENTS

THIS JOURNAL BELONGS TO	1
ABOUT YOUR JOURNAL	3
PERSONAL PRAYER GOALS	5
ABOUT THE AUTHOR	190
OTHER BOOKS FROM THE AUTHOR	191
CONTACT DETAILS	192
WORKS CITED	193
RECOMMENDED RESOURCES	194

ABOUT YOUR JOURNAL

"Then the LORD answered me and said, "Write the vision and engrave it plainly on [clay] tablets, so that the one who reads it will run."
Habakkuk 2:2

Prayer is communication with God, the Father, through the name of his son Jesus Christ, by the divine help of the Holy Spirit. This journal aims to inspire Christians to create a memory of their prayer walk, conversation, and experience with God during prayer.

The journal presents an inspiring personal diary and notebook, with space to write and record unique experiences with God Almighty. The journal encourages the Believer to create memories of their prayer life. Most importantly, it helps them define their prayer journey with actionable goals for future success.

The Journal gives the Believer, a unique opportunity to store key details of their prayer life. It provides a safe space to record memorable conversations with God, inspiring Believers to live out God's divine instructions as revealed to them in the place of prayer.

The word of God is an essential part of prayer, the journal, therefore, provides a space to record inspired Scriptures and Bible passages that come to heart during prayer.

One of the benefits of prayer is hearing God, the journal allows Believers to record revelations, prophecies, and words of knowledge revealed by God the Holy Spirit, during the quiet still moments of prayer.

There is a place to record inspired praise and worship songs, prayer requests, answered prayers or prayer testimonies, personal prayer notes for inner thoughts, feelings, passion rating and experiences in the spirit.

The journal provides sufficient space to write your vision and wisdom nuggets, ideas and action plans received during the prayer session for successful living.

"He has made everything beautiful and appropriate in its time. He has also planted eternity [a sense of divine purpose] in the human heart [a mysterious longing which nothing under the sun can satisfy, except God]—yet man cannot find out (comprehend, grasp) what God has done (His overall plan) from the beginning to the end."

ECCLESIASTES 3:11

PERSONAL PRAYER GOALS

___

___

___

___

___

___

___

___

___

___

"Call to Me and I will answer you and tell you [and even show you] great and mighty things, [things which have been confined and hidden], which you do not know and understand and cannot distinguish."

JEREMIAH 33:3

PRAYER NUGGETS

DATE _____

S M T W T F S

PRAISE & WORSHIP SONGS

PRAYER SCRIPTURES

WORD OF KNOWLEDGE

MEMORY VERSE

PRAYER REQUESTS

- ☐
- ☐
- ☐

PRAYER TESTIMONY

MY PASSION FOR PRAYER TODAY

☆ ☆ ☆ ☆ ☆

WISDOM NUGGETS

PRAYER ACTIONS

- ☐
- ☐
- ☐

NOTES

"But when you pray, go into your most private room, close the door, and pray to your Father who is in secret, and your Father who sees [what is done] in secret will reward you."

MATTHEW 6:6

PRAYER NUGGETS

DATE _____
S M T W T F S

PRAISE & WORSHIP SONGS

WORD OF KNOWLEDGE

PRAYER SCRIPTURES

MEMORY VERSE

PRAYER REQUESTS
- [ ]
- [ ]
- [ ]

WISDOM NUGGETS

PRAYER TESTIMONY

PRAYER ACTIONS
- [ ]
- [ ]
- [ ]

MY PASSION FOR PRAYER TODAY
☆ ☆ ☆ ☆ ☆

NOTES

"Be unceasing and persistent in prayer."

1 THESSALONIANS 5:17

PRAYER NUGGETS

DATE _____
S M T W T F S

PRAISE & WORSHIP SONGS

WORD OF KNOWLEDGE

PRAYER SCRIPTURES

MEMORY VERSE

PRAYER REQUESTS
- ☐
- ☐
- ☐

WISDOM NUGGETS

PRAYER TESTIMONY

PRAYER ACTIONS
- ☐
- ☐
- ☐

MY PASSION FOR PRAYER TODAY
☆ ☆ ☆ ☆ ☆

NOTES

"In the same way the Spirit [comes to us and] helps us in our weakness. We do not know what prayer to offer or how to offer it as we should, but the Spirit Himself [knows our need and at the right time] intercedes on our behalf with sighs and groanings too deep for words."

ROMANS 8:26

PRAYER NUGGETS

DATE _____

S M T W T F S

PRAISE & WORSHIP SONGS

WORD OF KNOWLEDGE

PRAYER SCRIPTURES

MEMORY VERSE

PRAYER REQUESTS

☐
☐
☐

WISDOM NUGGETS

PRAYER TESTIMONY

PRAYER ACTIONS

☐
☐
☐

MY PASSION FOR PRAYER TODAY

☆ ☆ ☆ ☆ ☆

NOTES

"And when you pray, do not use meaningless repetition as the Gentiles do, for they think they will be heard because of their many words."

MATTHEW 6:7

PRAYER NUGGETS

DATE _____
S M T W T F S

PRAISE & WORSHIP SONGS

WORD OF KNOWLEDGE

PRAYER SCRIPTURES

MEMORY VERSE

PRAYER REQUESTS
- [ ]
- [ ]
- [ ]

WISDOM NUGGETS

PRAYER TESTIMONY

PRAYER ACTIONS
- [ ]
- [ ]
- [ ]

MY PASSION FOR PRAYER TODAY
☆ ☆ ☆ ☆ ☆

NOTES

"So do not be like them [praying as they do]; for your Father knows what you need before you ask Him."

MATTHEW 6:8

PRAYER NUGGETS

DATE _____

S M T W T F S

PRAISE & WORSHIP SONGS

PRAYER SCRIPTURES

WORD OF KNOWLEDGE

MEMORY VERSE

PRAYER REQUESTS
- ☐
- ☐
- ☐

WISDOM NUGGETS

PRAYER TESTIMONY

PRAYER ACTIONS
- ☐
- ☐
- ☐

MY PASSION FOR PRAYER TODAY
☆ ☆ ☆ ☆ ☆

NOTES

"Pray, then, in this way: 'Our Father, who is in heaven, Hallowed be Your name.'"

MATTHEW 6:9

PRAYER NUGGETS

DATE _____
S M T W T F S

PRAISE & WORSHIP SONGS

WORD OF KNOWLEDGE

PRAYER SCRIPTURES

MEMORY VERSE

PRAYER REQUESTS
- ☐
- ☐
- ☐

WISDOM NUGGETS

PRAYER TESTIMONY

PRAYER ACTIONS
- ☐
- ☐
- ☐

MY PASSION FOR PRAYER TODAY
☆ ☆ ☆ ☆ ☆

NOTES

"With all prayer and petition always pray [with specific requests] [on every occasion and in every season] in the Spirit, and with this in view, stay alert with all perseverance and petition [interceding in prayer] for all God's people.

"EPHESIANS 6:18

PRAYER NUGGETS

DATE _____

S M T W T F S

PRAISE & WORSHIP SONGS

WORD OF KNOWLEDGE

PRAYER SCRIPTURES

MEMORY VERSE

PRAYER REQUESTS

- [ ]
- [ ]
- [ ]

WISDOM NUGGETS

PRAYER TESTIMONY

PRAYER ACTIONS

- [ ]
- [ ]
- [ ]

MY PASSION FOR PRAYER TODAY

☆ ☆ ☆ ☆ ☆

NOTES

"Therefore, confess your sins to one another [your false steps, your offenses], and pray for one another, that you may be healed and restored. The heartfelt and persistent prayer of a righteous man (believer) is able to accomplish much [when put into action and made effective by God—it is dynamic and can have tremendous power]."

JAMES 5:16

PRAYER NUGGETS

DATE _____

S   M   T   W   T   F   S

PRAISE & WORSHIP SONGS

PRAYER SCRIPTURES

WORD OF KNOWLEDGE

MEMORY VERSE

PRAYER REQUESTS
- ☐
- ☐
- ☐

PRAYER TESTIMONY

WISDOM NUGGETS

PRAYER ACTIONS
- ☐
- ☐
- ☐

MY PASSION FOR PRAYER TODAY
☆ ☆ ☆ ☆ ☆

NOTES

"Always giving thanks to God the Father for all things, in the name of our Lord Jesus Christ."

Ephesians 5:20

PRAYER NUGGETS

DATE _____
S M T W T F S

PRAISE & WORSHIP SONGS

WORD OF KNOWLEDGE

PRAYER SCRIPTURES

MEMORY VERSE

PRAYER REQUESTS
- ☐
- ☐
- ☐

WISDOM NUGGETS

PRAYER TESTIMONY

PRAYER ACTIONS
- ☐
- ☐
- ☐

MY PASSION FOR PRAYER TODAY
☆ ☆ ☆ ☆ ☆

NOTES

"For this reason, I am telling you, whatever things you ask for in prayer [in accordance with God's will], believe [with confident trust] that you have received them, and they will be given to you."

MARK 11:24

PRAYER NUGGETS

DATE _____
S M T W T F S

PRAISE & WORSHIP SONGS

WORD OF KNOWLEDGE

PRAYER SCRIPTURES

MEMORY VERSE

PRAYER REQUESTS
- ☐
- ☐
- ☐

WISDOM NUGGETS

PRAYER TESTIMONY

PRAYER ACTIONS
- ☐
- ☐
- ☐

MY PASSION FOR PRAYER TODAY
☆ ☆ ☆ ☆ ☆

NOTES

"This is the [remarkable degree of] confidence which we [as believers are entitled to] have before Him: that if we ask anything according to His will, [that is, consistent with His plan and purpose] He hears us."

1 JOHN 5:14

PRAYER NUGGETS

DATE _____

S M T W T F S

PRAISE & WORSHIP SONGS

WORD OF KNOWLEDGE

PRAYER SCRIPTURES

MEMORY VERSE

PRAYER REQUESTS
- ☐
- ☐
- ☐

WISDOM NUGGETS

PRAYER TESTIMONY

PRAYER ACTIONS
- ☐
- ☐
- ☐

MY PASSION FOR PRAYER TODAY
☆ ☆ ☆ ☆ ☆

NOTES

"Therefore, I want the men in every place to pray, lifting up holy hands, without anger and disputing or quarrelling or doubt [in their mind]."

1 TIMOTHY 2:8

PRAYER NUGGETS

DATE _____

S M T W T F S

PRAISE & WORSHIP SONGS

PRAYER SCRIPTURES

WORD OF KNOWLEDGE

MEMORY VERSE

PRAYER REQUESTS
- ☐
- ☐
- ☐

PRAYER TESTIMONY

WISDOM NUGGETS

PRAYER ACTIONS
- ☐
- ☐
- ☐

MY PASSION FOR PRAYER TODAY
☆ ☆ ☆ ☆ ☆

NOTES

"If you remain in Me and My words remain in you [that is, if we are vitally united and My message lives in your heart], ask whatever you wish, and it will be done for you."

JOHN 15:7

PRAYER NUGGETS

DATE _____
S M T W T F S

PRAISE & WORSHIP SONGS

WORD OF KNOWLEDGE

PRAYER SCRIPTURES

MEMORY VERSE

PRAYER REQUESTS
- ☐
- ☐
- ☐

WISDOM NUGGETS

PRAYER TESTIMONY

PRAYER ACTIONS
- ☐
- ☐
- ☐

MY PASSION FOR PRAYER TODAY
☆ ☆ ☆ ☆ ☆

NOTES

"You ask [God for something] and do not receive it, because you ask with wrong motives [out of selfishness or with an unrighteous agenda], so that [when you get what you want] you may spend it on your [hedonistic]" desires."

JAMES 4:3

PRAYER NUGGETS

DATE _____

S M T W T F S

PRAISE & WORSHIP SONGS

PRAYER SCRIPTURES

WORD OF KNOWLEDGE

MEMORY VERSE

PRAYER REQUESTS
- ☐
- ☐
- ☐

PRAYER TESTIMONY

WISDOM NUGGETS

PRAYER ACTIONS
- ☐
- ☐
- ☐

MY PASSION FOR PRAYER TODAY
☆ ☆ ☆ ☆ ☆

NOTES

"The LORD is near to all who call on Him, to all who call on Him in truth (without guile)."

PSALM 145:18

PRAYER NUGGETS

DATE _____

S M T W T F S

PRAISE & WORSHIP SONGS

PRAYER SCRIPTURES

WORD OF KNOWLEDGE

MEMORY VERSE

PRAYER REQUESTS
- [ ]
- [ ]
- [ ]

PRAYER TESTIMONY

WISDOM NUGGETS

PRAYER ACTIONS
- [ ]
- [ ]
- [ ]

MY PASSION FOR PRAYER TODAY
☆ ☆ ☆ ☆ ☆

NOTES

"If we [freely] admit that we have sinned and confess our sins, He is faithful and just [true to His own nature and promises] and will forgive our sins and cleanse us continually from all unrighteousness [our wrongdoing, everything not in conformity with His will and purpose]."

1 JOHN 1:9

PRAYER NUGGETS

DATE _____
S M T W T F S

PRAISE & WORSHIP SONGS

PRAYER SCRIPTURES

WORD OF KNOWLEDGE

MEMORY VERSE

PRAYER REQUESTS
- ☐
- ☐
- ☐

WISDOM NUGGETS

PRAYER TESTIMONY

PRAYER ACTIONS
- ☐
- ☐
- ☐

MY PASSION FOR PRAYER TODAY
☆ ☆ ☆ ☆ ☆

NOTES

"Therefore, let us [with privilege] approach the throne of grace [that is, the throne of God's gracious favour] with confidence and without fear, so that we may receive mercy [for our failures] and find [His amazing] grace to help in time of need [an appropriate blessing, coming just at the right moment]."

Hebrews 4:16

PRAYER NUGGETS

DATE _____

S M T W T F S

PRAISE & WORSHIP SONGS

WORD OF KNOWLEDGE

PRAYER SCRIPTURES

MEMORY VERSE

PRAYER REQUESTS
- ☐
- ☐
- ☐

WISDOM NUGGETS

PRAYER TESTIMONY

PRAYER ACTIONS
- ☐
- ☐
- ☐

MY PASSION FOR PRAYER TODAY
☆ ☆ ☆ ☆ ☆

NOTES

"Be persistent and devoted to prayer, being alert and focused on your prayer life with an attitude of thanksgiving."

COLOSSIANS 4:2

PRAYER NUGGETS

DATE _____
S M T W T F S

PRAISE & WORSHIP SONGS

WORD OF KNOWLEDGE

PRAYER SCRIPTURES

MEMORY VERSE

PRAYER REQUESTS
- ☐
- ☐
- ☐

WISDOM NUGGETS

PRAYER TESTIMONY

PRAYER ACTIONS
- ☐
- ☐
- ☐

MY PASSION FOR PRAYER TODAY
☆ ☆ ☆ ☆ ☆

NOTES

"Keep actively watching and praying that you may not come into temptation; the spirit is willing, but the body is weak."

MATTHEW 26:41

PRAYER NUGGETS

DATE _____

S M T W T F S

PRAISE & WORSHIP SONGS

WORD OF KNOWLEDGE

PRAYER SCRIPTURES

MEMORY VERSE

PRAYER REQUESTS
- ☐
- ☐
- ☐

WISDOM NUGGETS

PRAYER TESTIMONY

PRAYER ACTIONS
- ☐
- ☐
- ☐

MY PASSION FOR PRAYER TODAY
☆ ☆ ☆ ☆ ☆

NOTES

"Seek the LORD and His strength; Seek His face continually [longing to be in His presence]."

1 CHRONICLES 16:11

PRAYER NUGGETS

DATE _____
S M T W T F S

PRAISE & WORSHIP SONGS

PRAYER SCRIPTURES

WORD OF KNOWLEDGE

MEMORY VERSE

PRAYER REQUESTS
- ☐
- ☐
- ☐

WISDOM NUGGETS

PRAYER TESTIMONY

PRAYER ACTIONS
- ☐
- ☐
- ☐

MY PASSION FOR PRAYER TODAY
☆ ☆ ☆ ☆ ☆

NOTES

"Now at this time Jesus went off to the mountain to pray, and He spent the whole night in prayer to God."

LUKE 6:12

PRAYER NUGGETS

DATE _____

S M T W T F S

PRAISE & WORSHIP SONGS

WORD OF KNOWLEDGE

PRAYER SCRIPTURES

MEMORY VERSE

PRAYER REQUESTS
- ☐
- ☐
- ☐

WISDOM NUGGETS

PRAYER TESTIMONY

PRAYER ACTIONS
- ☐
- ☐
- ☐

MY PASSION FOR PRAYER TODAY
☆ ☆ ☆ ☆ ☆

NOTES

"And My people, who are called by My Name, humble themselves, and pray and seek (crave, require as a necessity) My face and turn from their wicked ways, then I will hear [them] from heaven, and forgive their sin and heal their land."

2 CHRONICLES 7:14

PRAYER NUGGETS

DATE _____
S M T W T F S

PRAISE & WORSHIP SONGS

WORD OF KNOWLEDGE

PRAYER SCRIPTURES

MEMORY VERSE

PRAYER REQUESTS
- ☐
- ☐
- ☐

WISDOM NUGGETS

PRAYER TESTIMONY

PRAYER ACTIONS
- ☐
- ☐
- ☐

MY PASSION FOR PRAYER TODAY
☆ ☆ ☆ ☆ ☆

NOTES

"Now Jesus was telling the disciples a parable to make the point that at all times they ought to pray and not give up and lose heart."

LUKE 18:1

PRAYER NUGGETS

DATE _____

S M T W T F S

PRAISE & WORSHIP SONGS

WORD OF KNOWLEDGE

PRAYER SCRIPTURES

MEMORY VERSE

PRAYER REQUESTS
- ☐
- ☐
- ☐

WISDOM NUGGETS

PRAYER TESTIMONY

PRAYER ACTIONS
- ☐
- ☐
- ☐

MY PASSION FOR PRAYER TODAY
☆ ☆ ☆ ☆ ☆

NOTES

"First of all, then, I urge that petitions (specific requests), prayers, intercessions (prayers for others) and thanksgivings be offered on behalf of all people, for kings and all who are in [positions of] high authority, so that we may live a peaceful and quiet life in all godliness and dignity."

1 TIMOTHY 2:1-2

PRAYER NUGGETS

DATE _____

S M T W T F S

PRAISE & WORSHIP SONGS

PRAYER SCRIPTURES

WORD OF KNOWLEDGE

MEMORY VERSE

PRAYER REQUESTS
- ☐
- ☐
- ☐

PRAYER TESTIMONY

MY PASSION FOR PRAYER TODAY
☆ ☆ ☆ ☆ ☆

WISDOM NUGGETS

PRAYER ACTIONS
- ☐
- ☐
- ☐

NOTES

"But I say to you, love [that is, unselfishly seek the best or higher good for] your enemies and pray for those who persecute you."

MATTHEW 5:44

PRAYER NUGGETS

DATE _____

S M T W T F S

PRAISE & WORSHIP SONGS

WORD OF KNOWLEDGE

PRAYER SCRIPTURES

MEMORY VERSE

PRAYER REQUESTS

- ☐
- ☐
- ☐

WISDOM NUGGETS

PRAYER TESTIMONY

PRAYER ACTIONS

- ☐
- ☐
- ☐

MY PASSION FOR PRAYER TODAY

☆ ☆ ☆ ☆ ☆

NOTES

"If any of you lacks wisdom [to guide him through a decision or circumstance], he is to ask of [our benevolent] God, who gives to everyone generously and without rebuke or blame, and it will be given to him."

JAMES 1:5

PRAYER NUGGETS

DATE _____
S M T W T F S

PRAISE & WORSHIP SONGS

WORD OF KNOWLEDGE

PRAYER SCRIPTURES

MEMORY VERSE

PRAYER REQUESTS
- ☐
- ☐
- ☐

WISDOM NUGGETS

PRAYER TESTIMONY

PRAYER ACTIONS
- ☐
- ☐
- ☐

MY PASSION FOR PRAYER TODAY
☆ ☆ ☆ ☆ ☆

NOTES

"Constantly rejoicing in hope [because of our confidence in Christ], steadfast and patient in distress, devoted to prayer [continually seeking wisdom, guidance, and strength]."

ROMANS 12:12

PRAYER NUGGETS

DATE _____

S M T W T F S

PRAISE & WORSHIP SONGS

WORD OF KNOWLEDGE

PRAYER SCRIPTURES

MEMORY VERSE

PRAYER REQUESTS

- [ ]
- [ ]
- [ ]

WISDOM NUGGETS

PRAYER TESTIMONY

PRAYER ACTIONS

- [ ]
- [ ]
- [ ]

MY PASSION FOR PRAYER TODAY

☆ ☆ ☆ ☆ ☆

NOTES

"He went away a second time and prayed, saying, "My Father, if this cannot pass away unless I drink it, your will be done."

MATTHEW 26:42

PRAYER NUGGETS

DATE _____

S M T W T F S

PRAISE & WORSHIP SONGS

WORD OF KNOWLEDGE

PRAYER SCRIPTURES

MEMORY VERSE

PRAYER REQUESTS

- [ ]
- [ ]
- [ ]

WISDOM NUGGETS

PRAYER TESTIMONY

PRAYER ACTIONS

- [ ]
- [ ]
- [ ]

MY PASSION FOR PRAYER TODAY
☆ ☆ ☆ ☆ ☆

NOTES

"Then you will call on Me and you will come and pray to Me, and I will hear [your voice] and I will listen to you."

JEREMIAH 29:12

PRAYER NUGGETS

DATE _____
S M T W T F S

PRAISE & WORSHIP SONGS

WORD OF KNOWLEDGE

PRAYER SCRIPTURES

MEMORY VERSE

PRAYER REQUESTS
- [ ]
- [ ]
- [ ]

WISDOM NUGGETS

PRAYER TESTIMONY

PRAYER ACTIONS
- [ ]
- [ ]

MY PASSION FOR PRAYER TODAY
☆ ☆ ☆ ☆ ☆

NOTES

"The LORD is far from the wicked [and distances Himself from them], But He hears the prayer of the [consistently] righteous [that is, those with spiritual integrity and moral courage]."

PROVERBS 15:29

PRAYER NUGGETS

DATE _____
S M T W T F S

PRAISE & WORSHIP SONGS

PRAYER SCRIPTURES

WORD OF KNOWLEDGE

MEMORY VERSE

PRAYER REQUESTS
- ☐
- ☐
- ☐

WISDOM NUGGETS

PRAYER TESTIMONY

PRAYER ACTIONS
- ☐
- ☐
- ☐

MY PASSION FOR PRAYER TODAY
☆ ☆ ☆ ☆ ☆

NOTES

"So, I say to you, ask and keep on asking, and it will be given to you; seek and keep on seeking, and you will find; knock and keep on knocking, and the door will be opened to you."

LUKE 11:9

PRAYER NUGGETS

DATE _____

S M T W T F S

PRAISE & WORSHIP SONGS

WORD OF KNOWLEDGE

PRAYER SCRIPTURES

MEMORY VERSE

PRAYER REQUESTS

- ☐
- ☐
- ☐

WISDOM NUGGETS

PRAYER TESTIMONY

PRAYER ACTIONS

- ☐
- ☐
- ☐

MY PASSION FOR PRAYER TODAY

☆ ☆ ☆ ☆ ☆

NOTES

"But he must ask [for wisdom] in faith, without doubting [God's willingness to help], for the one who doubts is like a billowing surge of the sea that is blown about and tossed by the wind."

JAMES 1:6

PRAYER NUGGETS

DATE _____

S M T W T F S

PRAISE & WORSHIP SONGS

WORD OF KNOWLEDGE

PRAYER SCRIPTURES

MEMORY VERSE

PRAYER REQUESTS

- [ ]
- [ ]
- [ ]

WISDOM NUGGETS

PRAYER TESTIMONY

PRAYER ACTIONS

- [ ]
- [ ]
- [ ]

MY PASSION FOR PRAYER TODAY

☆ ☆ ☆ ☆ ☆

NOTES

"All these with one mind and one purpose were continually devoting themselves to prayer, [waiting together] along with the women, and Mary the mother of Jesus, and with His brothers."

ACTS 1:14

PRAYER NUGGETS

DATE _____
S M T W T F S

PRAISE & WORSHIP SONGS

PRAYER SCRIPTURES

WORD OF KNOWLEDGE

MEMORY VERSE

PRAYER REQUESTS
- ☐
- ☐
- ☐

PRAYER TESTIMONY

WISDOM NUGGETS

PRAYER ACTIONS
- ☐
- ☐
- ☐

MY PASSION FOR PRAYER TODAY
☆ ☆ ☆ ☆ ☆

NOTES

"And whatever you ask for in prayer, believing, you will receive."

MATTHEW 21:22

PRAYER NUGGETS

DATE _____

S M T W T F S

PRAISE & WORSHIP SONGS

WORD OF KNOWLEDGE

PRAYER SCRIPTURES

MEMORY VERSE

PRAYER REQUESTS

- ☐
- ☐
- ☐

WISDOM NUGGETS

PRAYER TESTIMONY

PRAYER ACTIONS

- ☐
- ☐
- ☐

MY PASSION FOR PRAYER TODAY

☆ ☆ ☆ ☆ ☆

NOTES

"To the Chief Musician; on stringed instruments. A Psalm of David. Answer me when I call, O God of my righteousness! You have freed me when I was hemmed in and relieved me when I was in distress; Be gracious to me and hear [and respond to] my prayer."

PSALM 4:1

PRAYER NUGGETS

DATE _____
S M T W T F S

PRAISE & WORSHIP SONGS

WORD OF KNOWLEDGE

PRAYER SCRIPTURES

MEMORY VERSE

PRAYER REQUESTS
- ☐
- ☐
- ☐

WISDOM NUGGETS

PRAYER TESTIMONY

PRAYER ACTIONS
- ☐
- ☐
- ☐

MY PASSION FOR PRAYER TODAY
☆ ☆ ☆ ☆ ☆

NOTES

"And though one can overpower him who is alone, two can resist him. A cord of three strands is not quickly broken."

ECCLESIASTES 4:12

PRAYER NUGGETS

DATE _____
S M T W T F S

PRAISE & WORSHIP SONGS

WORD OF KNOWLEDGE

PRAYER SCRIPTURES

MEMORY VERSE

PRAYER REQUESTS
- [ ]
- [ ]
- [ ]

WISDOM NUGGETS

PRAYER TESTIMONY

PRAYER ACTIONS
- [ ]
- [ ]
- [ ]

MY PASSION FOR PRAYER TODAY
☆ ☆ ☆ ☆ ☆

NOTES

"If I regard sin and baseness in my heart [that is, if I know it is there and do nothing about it], The Lord will not hear [me]"

PSALM 66:18

PRAYER NUGGETS

DATE _____

S M T W T F S

PRAISE & WORSHIP SONGS

WORD OF KNOWLEDGE

PRAYER SCRIPTURES

MEMORY VERSE

PRAYER REQUESTS
- ☐
- ☐
- ☐

WISDOM NUGGETS

PRAYER TESTIMONY

PRAYER ACTIONS
- ☐
- ☐
- ☐

MY PASSION FOR PRAYER TODAY
☆ ☆ ☆ ☆ ☆

NOTES

"I assure you and most solemnly say to you, whatever you bind [forbid, declare to be improper and unlawful] on earth shall have [already] been bound in heaven, and whatever you loose [permit, declare lawful] on earth shall have [already] been loosed in heaven"

MATTHEW 18:18

PRAYER NUGGETS

DATE _____
S M T W T F S

PRAISE & WORSHIP SONGS

WORD OF KNOWLEDGE

PRAYER SCRIPTURES

MEMORY VERSE

PRAYER REQUESTS
- ☐
- ☐
- ☐

WISDOM NUGGETS

PRAYER TESTIMONY

PRAYER ACTIONS
- ☐
- ☐
- ☐

MY PASSION FOR PRAYER TODAY
☆ ☆ ☆ ☆ ☆

NOTES

"And do not lead us into temptation but deliver us from evil. [For Yours is the kingdom and the power and the glory forever. Amen.]"

MATTHEW 6:13

PRAYER NUGGETS

DATE _____

S M T W T F S

PRAISE & WORSHIP SONGS

WORD OF KNOWLEDGE

PRAYER SCRIPTURES

MEMORY VERSE

PRAYER REQUESTS
- [ ]
- [ ]
- [ ]

WISDOM NUGGETS

PRAYER TESTIMONY

PRAYER ACTIONS
- [ ]
- [ ]
- [ ]

MY PASSION FOR PRAYER TODAY
☆ ☆ ☆ ☆ ☆

NOTES

"I cried aloud to Him; He was highly praised with my tongue."

Psalm 66:17

PRAYER NUGGETS

DATE _____

S M T W T F S

PRAISE & WORSHIP SONGS

PRAYER SCRIPTURES

WORD OF KNOWLEDGE

MEMORY VERSE

PRAYER REQUESTS
- [ ]
- [ ]
- [ ]

PRAYER TESTIMONY

WISDOM NUGGETS

PRAYER ACTIONS
- [ ]
- [ ]
- [ ]

MY PASSION FOR PRAYER TODAY
☆ ☆ ☆ ☆ ☆

NOTES

"Pray for the peace of Jerusalem: "May they prosper who love you [holy city]."

Psalm 122:6

PRAYER NUGGETS

DATE _____

S M T W T F S

PRAISE & WORSHIP SONGS

PRAYER SCRIPTURES

WORD OF KNOWLEDGE

MEMORY VERSE

PRAYER REQUESTS
- [ ]
- [ ]
- [ ]

PRAYER TESTIMONY

WISDOM NUGGETS

PRAYER ACTIONS
- [ ]
- [ ]
- [ ]

MY PASSION FOR PRAYER TODAY
☆ ☆ ☆ ☆ ☆

NOTES

"And if we know [for a fact, as indeed we do] that He hears and listens to us in whatever we ask, we [also] know [with settled and absolute knowledge] that we have [granted to us] the requests which we have asked from Him."

1 JOHN 5:15

PRAYER NUGGETS

DATE _____

S M T W T F S

PRAISE & WORSHIP SONGS

WORD OF KNOWLEDGE

PRAYER SCRIPTURES

MEMORY VERSE

PRAYER REQUESTS
- ☐
- ☐
- ☐

WISDOM NUGGETS

PRAYER TESTIMONY

PRAYER ACTIONS
- ☐
- ☐
- ☐

MY PASSION FOR PRAYER TODAY
☆ ☆ ☆ ☆ ☆

NOTES

"I pray for them; I do not pray for the world, but for those You have given Me, because they belong to You."

JOHN 17:9

PRAYER NUGGETS

DATE _____

S M T W T F S

PRAISE & WORSHIP SONGS

PRAYER SCRIPTURES

WORD OF KNOWLEDGE

MEMORY VERSE

PRAYER REQUESTS
- [ ]
- [ ]
- [ ]

PRAYER TESTIMONY

WISDOM NUGGETS

PRAYER ACTIONS
- [ ]
- [ ]
- [ ]

MY PASSION FOR PRAYER TODAY
☆ ☆ ☆ ☆ ☆

NOTES

"And I will do whatever you ask in My name [as My representative], this I will do, so that the Father may be glorified and celebrated in the Son. If you ask Me anything in My name [as My representative], I will do it."

JOHN 14:13

PRAYER NUGGETS

DATE _____

S M T W T F S

PRAISE & WORSHIP SONGS

PRAYER SCRIPTURES

WORD OF KNOWLEDGE

MEMORY VERSE

PRAYER REQUESTS
- ☐
- ☐
- ☐

PRAYER TESTIMONY

WISDOM NUGGETS

PRAYER ACTIONS
- ☐
- ☐
- ☐

MY PASSION FOR PRAYER TODAY
☆ ☆ ☆ ☆ ☆

NOTES

"And we know [with great confidence] that God [who is deeply concerned about us] causes all things to work together [as a plan] for good for those who love God, to those who are called according to His plan and purpose."

ROMANS 8:28

PRAYER NUGGETS

DATE _____
S M T W T F S

PRAISE & WORSHIP SONGS

WORD OF KNOWLEDGE

PRAYER SCRIPTURES

MEMORY VERSE

PRAYER REQUESTS
- ☐
- ☐
- ☐

WISDOM NUGGETS

PRAYER TESTIMONY

PRAYER ACTIONS
- ☐
- ☐
- ☐

MY PASSION FOR PRAYER TODAY
☆ ☆ ☆ ☆ ☆

NOTES

"Let my prayer be counted as incense before You; The lifting up of my hands as the evening offering."

PSALM 141:2

PRAYER NUGGETS

DATE _____
S M T W T F S

PRAISE & WORSHIP SONGS

WORD OF KNOWLEDGE

PRAYER SCRIPTURES

MEMORY VERSE

PRAYER REQUESTS
- ☐
- ☐
- ☐

WISDOM NUGGETS

PRAYER TESTIMONY

PRAYER ACTIONS
- ☐
- ☐
- ☐

MY PASSION FOR PRAYER TODAY
☆ ☆ ☆ ☆ ☆

NOTES

"For there is [only] one God, and [only] one Mediator between God and mankind, the Man Christ Jesus."

1 Timothy 2:5

PRAYER NUGGETS

DATE _____

S M T W T F S

PRAISE & WORSHIP SONGS

WORD OF KNOWLEDGE

PRAYER SCRIPTURES

MEMORY VERSE

PRAYER REQUESTS

- ☐
- ☐
- ☐

WISDOM NUGGETS

PRAYER TESTIMONY

PRAYER ACTIONS

- ☐
- ☐
- ☐

MY PASSION FOR PRAYER TODAY

☆ ☆ ☆ ☆ ☆

NOTES

"The name of the LORD is a strong tower; The righteous runs to it and is safe and set on high [far above evil]."

PROVERBS 18:10

PRAYER NUGGETS

DATE _____
S M T W T F S

PRAISE & WORSHIP SONGS

WORD OF KNOWLEDGE

PRAYER SCRIPTURES

MEMORY VERSE

PRAYER REQUESTS
- ☐
- ☐
- ☐

WISDOM NUGGETS

PRAYER TESTIMONY

PRAYER ACTIONS
- ☐
- ☐
- ☐

MY PASSION FOR PRAYER TODAY
☆ ☆ ☆ ☆ ☆

NOTES

"Bless and show kindness to those who curse you, pray for those who mistreat you."

LUKE 6:28

PRAYER NUGGETS

DATE _____

S M T W T F S

PRAISE & WORSHIP SONGS

WORD OF KNOWLEDGE

PRAYER SCRIPTURES

MEMORY VERSE

PRAYER REQUESTS
- [ ]
- [ ]
- [ ]

WISDOM NUGGETS

PRAYER TESTIMONY

PRAYER ACTIONS
- [ ]
- [ ]
- [ ]

MY PASSION FOR PRAYER TODAY
☆ ☆ ☆ ☆ ☆

NOTES

"Delight yourself in the LORD, And He will give you the desires and petitions of your heart."

Psalm 37:4

PRAYER NUGGETS

DATE _____

S M T W T F S

PRAISE & WORSHIP SONGS

PRAYER SCRIPTURES

WORD OF KNOWLEDGE

MEMORY VERSE

PRAYER REQUESTS

- [ ]
- [ ]
- [ ]

PRAYER TESTIMONY

WISDOM NUGGETS

PRAYER ACTIONS

- [ ]
- [ ]
- [ ]

MY PASSION FOR PRAYER TODAY

☆ ☆ ☆ ☆ ☆

NOTES

"The eyes of the LORD are toward the righteous [those with moral courage and spiritual integrity] And His ears are open to their cry."

PSALM 34:15

PRAYER NUGGETS

DATE _____

S M T W T F S

PRAISE & WORSHIP SONGS

WORD OF KNOWLEDGE

PRAYER SCRIPTURES

MEMORY VERSE

PRAYER REQUESTS

☐
☐
☐

WISDOM NUGGETS

PRAYER TESTIMONY

PRAYER ACTIONS

☐
☐
☐

MY PASSION FOR PRAYER TODAY
☆ ☆ ☆ ☆ ☆

NOTES

"I called to the LORD in my distress, and I cried to my God for help. From his temple he heard my voice, and my cry to him reached his ears."

PSALM 18:6

PRAYER NUGGETS

DATE _____

S M T W T F S

PRAISE & WORSHIP SONGS

PRAYER SCRIPTURES

WORD OF KNOWLEDGE

MEMORY VERSE

PRAYER REQUESTS

- ☐
- ☐
- ☐

PRAYER TESTIMONY

WISDOM NUGGETS

PRAYER ACTIONS

- ☐
- ☐
- ☐

MY PASSION FOR PRAYER TODAY

☆ ☆ ☆ ☆ ☆

NOTES

"Ask and keep on asking and it will be given to you; seek and keep on seeking and you will find; knock and keep on knocking and the door will be opened to you."

MATTHEW 7:7

PRAYER NUGGETS

DATE _____

S M T W T F S

PRAISE & WORSHIP SONGS

PRAYER SCRIPTURES

WORD OF KNOWLEDGE

MEMORY VERSE

PRAYER REQUESTS
- ☐
- ☐
- ☐

WISDOM NUGGETS

PRAYER TESTIMONY

PRAYER ACTIONS
- ☐
- ☐
- ☐

MY PASSION FOR PRAYER TODAY
☆ ☆ ☆ ☆ ☆

NOTES

"Evening and morning and at noon I will complain and murmur, And He will hear my voice."

PSALM 55:17

PRAYER NUGGETS

DATE _____
S M T W T F S

PRAISE & WORSHIP SONGS

PRAYER SCRIPTURES

WORD OF KNOWLEDGE

MEMORY VERSE

PRAYER REQUESTS
- ☐
- ☐
- ☐

WISDOM NUGGETS

PRAYER TESTIMONY

PRAYER ACTIONS
- ☐
- ☐
- ☐

MY PASSION FOR PRAYER TODAY
☆ ☆ ☆ ☆ ☆

NOTES

"Is anyone among you suffering? He must pray. Is anyone joyful? He is to sing praises [to God]."

JAMES 5:13

PRAYER NUGGETS

DATE _____
S M T W T F S

PRAISE & WORSHIP SONGS

PRAYER SCRIPTURES

WORD OF KNOWLEDGE

MEMORY VERSE

PRAYER REQUESTS
- ☐
- ☐
- ☐

PRAYER TESTIMONY

WISDOM NUGGETS

PRAYER ACTIONS
- ☐
- ☐
- ☐

MY PASSION FOR PRAYER TODAY
☆ ☆ ☆ ☆ ☆

NOTES

"But Peter sent them all out [of the room] and knelt down and prayed; then turning to the body he said, "Tabitha, arise!" And she opened her eyes, and when she saw Peter, she sat up."

ACTS 9:40

PRAYER NUGGETS

DATE _____

S M T W T F S

PRAISE & WORSHIP SONGS

PRAYER SCRIPTURES

WORD OF KNOWLEDGE

MEMORY VERSE

PRAYER REQUESTS
- ☐
- ☐
- ☐

PRAYER TESTIMONY

WISDOM NUGGETS

PRAYER ACTIONS
- ☐
- ☐
- ☐

MY PASSION FOR PRAYER TODAY
☆ ☆ ☆ ☆ ☆

NOTES

"If you then, evil (sinful by nature) as you are, know how to give good and advantageous gifts to your children, how much more will your Father who is in heaven [perfect as He is] give what is good and advantageous to those who keep on asking Him."

MATTHEW 7:11

PRAYER NUGGETS

DATE _____

S M T W T F S

PRAISE & WORSHIP SONGS

PRAYER SCRIPTURES

WORD OF KNOWLEDGE

MEMORY VERSE

PRAYER REQUESTS
- [ ]
- [ ]
- [ ]

PRAYER TESTIMONY

WISDOM NUGGETS

PRAYER ACTIONS
- [ ]
- [ ]
- [ ]

MY PASSION FOR PRAYER TODAY
☆ ☆ ☆ ☆ ☆

NOTES

"So, submit to [the authority of] God. Resist the devil [stand firm against him] and he will flee from you."

JAMES 4:7

PRAYER NUGGETS

DATE _____
S M T W T F S

PRAISE & WORSHIP SONGS

PRAYER SCRIPTURES

WORD OF KNOWLEDGE

MEMORY VERSE

PRAYER REQUESTS
- ☐
- ☐
- ☐

WISDOM NUGGETS

PRAYER TESTIMONY

PRAYER ACTIONS
- ☐
- ☐
- ☐

MY PASSION FOR PRAYER TODAY
☆ ☆ ☆ ☆ ☆

NOTES

"Now faith is the assurance (title deed, confirmation) of things hoped for (divinely guaranteed), and the evidence of things not seen [the conviction of their reality—faith comprehends as fact what cannot be experienced by the physical senses]."

HEBREWS 11:1

PRAYER NUGGETS

DATE _____

S M T W T F S

PRAISE & WORSHIP SONGS

PRAYER SCRIPTURES

WORD OF KNOWLEDGE

MEMORY VERSE

PRAYER REQUESTS
- ☐
- ☐
- ☐

WISDOM NUGGETS

PRAYER TESTIMONY

PRAYER ACTIONS
- ☐
- ☐
- ☐

MY PASSION FOR PRAYER TODAY
☆ ☆ ☆ ☆ ☆

NOTES

"O LORD, save now, we beseech You; O LORD, we beseech You, send now prosperity and give us success!"

PSALM 118:25

PRAYER NUGGETS

DATE _____
S M T W T F S

PRAISE & WORSHIP SONGS

WORD OF KNOWLEDGE

PRAYER SCRIPTURES

MEMORY VERSE

PRAYER REQUESTS
- ☐
- ☐
- ☐

WISDOM NUGGETS

PRAYER TESTIMONY

PRAYER ACTIONS
- ☐
- ☐
- ☐

MY PASSION FOR PRAYER TODAY
☆ ☆ ☆ ☆ ☆

NOTES

"A Psalm of David. The LORD is my Shepherd [to feed, to guide and to shield me], I shall not want."

PSALM 23:1

PRAYER NUGGETS

DATE _____
S M T W T F S

PRAISE & WORSHIP SONGS

PRAYER SCRIPTURES

WORD OF KNOWLEDGE

MEMORY VERSE

PRAYER REQUESTS
- ☐
- ☐
- ☐

PRAYER TESTIMONY

WISDOM NUGGETS

PRAYER ACTIONS
- ☐
- ☐
- ☐

MY PASSION FOR PRAYER TODAY
☆ ☆ ☆ ☆ ☆

NOTES

"And we receive from Him whatever we ask because we [carefully and consistently] keep His commandments and do the things that are pleasing in His sight [habitually seeking to follow His plan for us]."

1 JOHN 3:22

PRAYER NUGGETS

DATE _____
S M T W T F S

PRAISE & WORSHIP SONGS

WORD OF KNOWLEDGE

PRAYER SCRIPTURES

MEMORY VERSE

PRAYER REQUESTS
- ☐
- ☐
- ☐

WISDOM NUGGETS

PRAYER TESTIMONY

PRAYER ACTIONS
- ☐
- ☐
- ☐

MY PASSION FOR PRAYER TODAY
☆ ☆ ☆ ☆ ☆

NOTES

"Do not be anxious or worried about anything, but in everything [every circumstance and situation] by prayer and petition with thanksgiving, continue to make your [specific] requests known to God."

PHILIPPIANS 4:6

PRAYER NUGGETS

DATE _____
S M T W T F S

PRAISE & WORSHIP SONGS

PRAYER SCRIPTURES

WORD OF KNOWLEDGE

MEMORY VERSE

PRAYER REQUESTS
- ☐
- ☐
- ☐

PRAYER TESTIMONY

WISDOM NUGGETS

PRAYER ACTIONS
- ☐
- ☐
- ☐

MY PASSION FOR PRAYER TODAY
☆ ☆ ☆ ☆ ☆

NOTES

"And whatever you ask for in prayer, believing, you will receive."

MATTHEW 21:22

PRAYER NUGGETS

DATE _____
S M T W T F S

PRAISE & WORSHIP SONGS

PRAYER SCRIPTURES

WORD OF KNOWLEDGE

MEMORY VERSE

PRAYER REQUESTS
- [ ]
- [ ]
- [ ]

PRAYER TESTIMONY

WISDOM NUGGETS

PRAYER ACTIONS
- [ ]
- [ ]
- [ ]

MY PASSION FOR PRAYER TODAY
☆ ☆ ☆ ☆ ☆

NOTES

"But without faith it is impossible to [walk with God and] please Him, for whoever comes [near] to God must [necessarily] believe that God exists and that He rewards those who [earnestly and diligently] seek Him."

Hebrews 11:6

PRAYER NUGGETS

DATE _____

S M T W T F S

PRAISE & WORSHIP SONGS

WORD OF KNOWLEDGE

PRAYER SCRIPTURES

MEMORY VERSE

PRAYER REQUESTS
- ☐
- ☐
- ☐

WISDOM NUGGETS

PRAYER TESTIMONY

PRAYER ACTIONS
- ☐
- ☐
- ☐

MY PASSION FOR PRAYER TODAY
☆ ☆ ☆ ☆ ☆

NOTES

"Jesus replied, "Have faith in God [constantly]."

MARK 11:22

PRAYER NUGGETS

DATE _____

S M T W T F S

PRAISE & WORSHIP SONGS

PRAYER SCRIPTURES

WORD OF KNOWLEDGE

MEMORY VERSE

PRAYER REQUESTS
- [ ]
- [ ]
- [ ]

PRAYER TESTIMONY

WISDOM NUGGETS

PRAYER ACTIONS
- [ ]
- [ ]

MY PASSION FOR PRAYER TODAY
☆ ☆ ☆ ☆ ☆

NOTES

"I assure you and most solemnly say to you, whoever says to this mountain, 'Be lifted up and thrown into the sea!' and does not doubt in his heart [in God's unlimited power] but believes that what he says is going to take place, it will be done for him [in accordance with God's will]."

MARK 11:23

PRAYER NUGGETS

DATE _____

S M T W T F S

PRAISE & WORSHIP SONGS

PRAYER SCRIPTURES

WORD OF KNOWLEDGE

MEMORY VERSE

PRAYER REQUESTS

- ☐
- ☐
- ☐

PRAYER TESTIMONY

WISDOM NUGGETS

PRAYER ACTIONS

- ☐
- ☐
- ☐

MY PASSION FOR PRAYER TODAY

☆ ☆ ☆ ☆ ☆

NOTES

"For with God nothing [is or ever] shall be impossible."

LUKE 1:37

PRAYER NUGGETS

DATE _____

S M T W T F S

PRAISE & WORSHIP SONGS

WORD OF KNOWLEDGE

PRAYER SCRIPTURES

MEMORY VERSE

PRAYER REQUESTS

☐
☐
☐

WISDOM NUGGETS

PRAYER TESTIMONY

PRAYER ACTIONS

☐
☐
☐

MY PASSION FOR PRAYER TODAY

☆ ☆ ☆ ☆ ☆

NOTES

"Trust in and rely confidently on the LORD with all your heart and do not rely on your own insight or understanding, in all your ways know and acknowledge and recognize Him, And He will make your paths straight and smooth [removing obstacles that block your way]."

PROVERBS 3:5-6

PRAYER NUGGETS

DATE _____

S M T W T F S

PRAISE & WORSHIP SONGS

WORD OF KNOWLEDGE

PRAYER SCRIPTURES

MEMORY VERSE

PRAYER REQUESTS
- ☐
- ☐
- ☐

WISDOM NUGGETS

PRAYER TESTIMONY

PRAYER ACTIONS
- ☐
- ☐
- ☐

MY PASSION FOR PRAYER TODAY
☆ ☆ ☆ ☆ ☆

NOTES

"So that your faith would not rest on the wisdom and rhetoric of men, but on the power of God."

1 CORINTHIANS 2:5

PRAYER NUGGETS

DATE _____
S M T W T F S

PRAISE & WORSHIP SONGS

PRAYER SCRIPTURES

WORD OF KNOWLEDGE

MEMORY VERSE

PRAYER REQUESTS
- ☐
- ☐
- ☐

WISDOM NUGGETS

PRAYER TESTIMONY

PRAYER ACTIONS
- ☐
- ☐
- ☐

MY PASSION FOR PRAYER TODAY
☆ ☆ ☆ ☆ ☆

NOTES

"For it is by grace [God's remarkable compassion and favour drawing you to Christ] that you have been saved [delivered from judgment and given eternal life] through faith. And this [salvation] is not of yourselves [not through your own effort], but it is the [undeserved, gracious] gift of God."

EPHESIANS 2:8

PRAYER NUGGETS

DATE _____

S M T W T F S

PRAISE & WORSHIP SONGS

WORD OF KNOWLEDGE

PRAYER SCRIPTURES

MEMORY VERSE

PRAYER REQUESTS

- ☐
- ☐
- ☐

WISDOM NUGGETS

PRAYER TESTIMONY

PRAYER ACTIONS

- ☐
- ☐
- ☐

MY PASSION FOR PRAYER TODAY

☆ ☆ ☆ ☆ ☆

NOTES

"Above all, lift up the [protective] shield of faith with which you can extinguish all the flaming arrows of the evil one."

Ephesians 6:16

PRAYER NUGGETS

DATE _____
S M T W T F S

PRAISE & WORSHIP SONGS

PRAYER SCRIPTURES

WORD OF KNOWLEDGE

MEMORY VERSE

PRAYER REQUESTS
- ☐
- ☐
- ☐

PRAYER TESTIMONY

WISDOM NUGGETS

PRAYER ACTIONS
- ☐
- ☐
- ☐

MY PASSION FOR PRAYER TODAY
☆ ☆ ☆ ☆ ☆

NOTES

"And take THE HELMET OF SALVATION, and the sword of the Spirit, which is the Word of God."

Ephesians 6:17

PRAYER NUGGETS

DATE _____

S M T W T F S

PRAISE & WORSHIP SONGS

WORD OF KNOWLEDGE

PRAYER SCRIPTURES

MEMORY VERSE

PRAYER REQUESTS
- ☐
- ☐
- ☐

WISDOM NUGGETS

PRAYER TESTIMONY

PRAYER ACTIONS
- ☐
- ☐
- ☐

MY PASSION FOR PRAYER TODAY
☆ ☆ ☆ ☆ ☆

NOTES

"Be sober [well balanced and self-disciplined], be always alert and cautious. That enemy of yours, the devil, prowls around like a roaring lion [fiercely hungry], seeking someone to devour."

1 Peter 5:8

PRAYER NUGGETS

DATE _____
S M T W T F S

PRAISE & WORSHIP SONGS

WORD OF KNOWLEDGE

PRAYER SCRIPTURES

MEMORY VERSE

PRAYER REQUESTS
- ☐
- ☐
- ☐

WISDOM NUGGETS

PRAYER TESTIMONY

PRAYER ACTIONS
- ☐
- ☐
- ☐

MY PASSION FOR PRAYER TODAY
☆ ☆ ☆ ☆ ☆

NOTES

"But resist him, be firm in your faith [against his attack—rooted, established, immovable], knowing that the same experiences of suffering are being experienced by your brothers and sisters throughout the world. [You do not suffer alone.]"

1 Peter 5:9

PRAYER NUGGETS

DATE _____

S M T W T F S

PRAISE & WORSHIP SONGS

PRAYER SCRIPTURES

WORD OF KNOWLEDGE

MEMORY VERSE

PRAYER REQUESTS

- ☐
- ☐
- ☐

PRAYER TESTIMONY

WISDOM NUGGETS

PRAYER ACTIONS

- ☐
- ☐
- ☐

MY PASSION FOR PRAYER TODAY

☆ ☆ ☆ ☆ ☆

NOTES

"And the peace of God [that peace which reassures the heart, that peace] which transcends all understanding, [that peace which] stands guard over your hearts and your minds in Christ Jesus [is yours]."

PHILIPPIANS 4:7

PRAYER NUGGETS

DATE _____
S M T W T F S

PRAISE & WORSHIP SONGS

WORD OF KNOWLEDGE

PRAYER SCRIPTURES

MEMORY VERSE

PRAYER REQUESTS
- ☐
- ☐
- ☐

WISDOM NUGGETS

PRAYER TESTIMONY

PRAYER ACTIONS
- ☐
- ☐
- ☐

MY PASSION FOR PRAYER TODAY
☆ ☆ ☆ ☆ ☆

NOTES

"I can do all things [which He has called me to do] through Him who strengthens and empowers me [to fulfill His purpose—I am self-sufficient in Christ's sufficiency; I am ready for anything and equal to anything through Him who infuses me with inner strength and confident peace.]"

PHILIPPIANS 4:13

PRAYER NUGGETS

DATE _____

S M T W T F S

PRAISE & WORSHIP SONGS

WORD OF KNOWLEDGE

PRAYER SCRIPTURES

MEMORY VERSE

PRAYER REQUESTS
- ☐
- ☐
- ☐

WISDOM NUGGETS

PRAYER TESTIMONY

PRAYER ACTIONS
- ☐
- ☐
- ☐

MY PASSION FOR PRAYER TODAY
☆ ☆ ☆ ☆ ☆

NOTES

"And my God will liberally supply (fill until full) your every need according to His riches in glory in Christ Jesus."

PHILIPPIANS 4:19

PRAYER NUGGETS

DATE _____
S M T W T F S

PRAISE & WORSHIP SONGS

WORD OF KNOWLEDGE

PRAYER SCRIPTURES

MEMORY VERSE

PRAYER REQUESTS
- [ ]
- [ ]
- [ ]

WISDOM NUGGETS

PRAYER TESTIMONY

PRAYER ACTIONS
- [ ]
- [ ]
- [ ]

MY PASSION FOR PRAYER TODAY
☆ ☆ ☆ ☆ ☆

NOTES

"But He has said to me, "My grace is sufficient for you [My lovingkindness and My mercy are more than enough—always available—regardless of the situation]; for [My] power is being perfected [and is completed and shows itself most effectively] in [your] weakness. Therefore, I will even more gladly boast in my weaknesses, so that the power of Christ [may completely enfold me and] may dwell in me."

2 CORINTHIANS 12:9

PRAYER NUGGETS

DATE _____
S M T W T F S

PRAISE & WORSHIP SONGS

PRAYER SCRIPTURES

WORD OF KNOWLEDGE

MEMORY VERSE

PRAYER REQUESTS
- ☐
- ☐
- ☐

PRAYER TESTIMONY

WISDOM NUGGETS

PRAYER ACTIONS
- ☐
- ☐
- ☐

MY PASSION FOR PRAYER TODAY
☆ ☆ ☆ ☆ ☆

NOTES

"A Song of Ascents. I will lift up my eyes to the hills [of Jerusalem]— From where my help shall come? My help comes from the LORD, who made heaven and earth. He will not allow your foot to slip; He who keeps you will not slumber."

PSALM 121:1-3

PRAYER NUGGETS

DATE _____
S M T W T F S

PRAISE & WORSHIP SONGS

WORD OF KNOWLEDGE

PRAYER SCRIPTURES

MEMORY VERSE

PRAYER REQUESTS
- ☐
- ☐
- ☐

WISDOM NUGGETS

PRAYER TESTIMONY

PRAYER ACTIONS
- ☐
- ☐
- ☐

MY PASSION FOR PRAYER TODAY
☆ ☆ ☆ ☆ ☆

NOTES

"Let your character [your moral essence, your inner nature] be free from the love of money [shun greed—be financially ethical], being content with what you have; for He has said, "I WILL NEVER [under any circumstances] DESERT YOU [nor give you up nor leave you without support, nor will I in any degree leave you helpless], NOR WILL I FORSAKE *or* LET YOU DOWN *or* RELAX MY HOLD ON YOU [assuredly not]!"

HEBREWS 13:5

PRAYER NUGGETS

DATE _____

S M T W T F S

PRAISE & WORSHIP SONGS

WORD OF KNOWLEDGE

PRAYER SCRIPTURES

MEMORY VERSE

PRAYER REQUESTS

☐
☐
☐

WISDOM NUGGETS

PRAYER TESTIMONY

PRAYER ACTIONS

☐
☐
☐

MY PASSION FOR PRAYER TODAY

☆ ☆ ☆ ☆ ☆

NOTES

"You shall love the LORD your God with all your heart and mind and with all your soul and with all your strength [your entire being]."

DEUTERONOMY 6:5

PRAYER NUGGETS

DATE _____
S M T W T F S

PRAISE & WORSHIP SONGS

PRAYER SCRIPTURES

WORD OF KNOWLEDGE

MEMORY VERSE

PRAYER REQUESTS
- [ ]
- [ ]
- [ ]

PRAYER TESTIMONY

WISDOM NUGGETS

PRAYER ACTIONS
- [ ]
- [ ]
- [ ]

MY PASSION FOR PRAYER TODAY
☆ ☆ ☆ ☆ ☆

NOTES

"A Song of Ascents. Of Solomon. Unless the LORD builds the house, they labour in vain who build it; Unless the LORD guards the city, The watchman keeps awake in vain."

PSALM 127:1

PRAYER NUGGETS

DATE _____

S M T W T F S

PRAISE & WORSHIP SONGS

WORD OF KNOWLEDGE

PRAYER SCRIPTURES

MEMORY VERSE

PRAYER REQUESTS
- [ ]
- [ ]
- [ ]

WISDOM NUGGETS

PRAYER TESTIMONY

PRAYER ACTIONS
- [ ]
- [ ]
- [ ]

MY PASSION FOR PRAYER TODAY
☆ ☆ ☆ ☆ ☆

NOTES

"I, the LORD, am its Keeper; I water it every moment. So that no one will harm it, I guard it night and day."

ISAIAH 27:3

PRAYER NUGGETS

DATE _____

S M T W T F S

PRAISE & WORSHIP SONGS

WORD OF KNOWLEDGE

PRAYER SCRIPTURES

MEMORY VERSE

PRAYER REQUESTS

- ☐
- ☐
- ☐

WISDOM NUGGETS

PRAYER TESTIMONY

PRAYER ACTIONS

- ☐
- ☐
- ☐

MY PASSION FOR PRAYER TODAY

☆ ☆ ☆ ☆ ☆

NOTES

"For He will command His angels in regard to you, to protect and defend and guard you in all your ways [of obedience and service]."

PSALM 91:11

PRAYER NUGGETS

DATE _____
S M T W T F S

PRAISE & WORSHIP SONGS

WORD OF KNOWLEDGE

PRAYER SCRIPTURES

MEMORY VERSE

PRAYER REQUESTS
- ☐
- ☐
- ☐

WISDOM NUGGETS

PRAYER TESTIMONY

PRAYER ACTIONS
- ☐
- ☐
- ☐

MY PASSION FOR PRAYER TODAY
☆ ☆ ☆ ☆ ☆

NOTES

"Elisha answered, "Do not be afraid, for those who are with us are more than those who are with them."

2 KINGS 6:16

PRAYER NUGGETS

DATE _____
S M T W T F S

PRAISE & WORSHIP SONGS

PRAYER SCRIPTURES

WORD OF KNOWLEDGE

MEMORY VERSE

PRAYER REQUESTS
- ☐
- ☐
- ☐

PRAYER TESTIMONY

WISDOM NUGGETS

PRAYER ACTIONS
- ☐
- ☐
- ☐

MY PASSION FOR PRAYER TODAY
☆ ☆ ☆ ☆ ☆

NOTES

"Arise [from spiritual depression to a new life], shine [be radiant with the glory and brilliance of the LORD]; for your light has come, And the glory and brilliance of the LORD has risen upon you."

ISAIAH 60:1

PRAYER NUGGETS

DATE _____
S M T W T F S

PRAISE & WORSHIP SONGS

WORD OF KNOWLEDGE

PRAYER SCRIPTURES

MEMORY VERSE

PRAYER REQUESTS
- ☐
- ☐
- ☐

WISDOM NUGGETS

PRAYER TESTIMONY

PRAYER ACTIONS
- ☐
- ☐
- ☐

MY PASSION FOR PRAYER TODAY
☆ ☆ ☆ ☆ ☆

NOTES

"For in fact, darkness will cover the earth and deep darkness will cover the peoples; But the LORD will rise upon you [Jerusalem] And His glory and brilliance will be seen on you."

ISAIAH 60:2

PRAYER NUGGETS

DATE _____
S M T W T F S

PRAISE & WORSHIP SONGS

WORD OF KNOWLEDGE

PRAYER SCRIPTURES

MEMORY VERSE

PRAYER REQUESTS
- ☐
- ☐
- ☐

WISDOM NUGGETS

PRAYER TESTIMONY

PRAYER ACTIONS
- ☐
- ☐
- ☐

MY PASSION FOR PRAYER TODAY
☆ ☆ ☆ ☆ ☆

NOTES

"Again, I say to you, that if two believers on earth agree [that is, are of one mind, in harmony] about anything that they ask [within the will of God], it will be done for them by My Father in heaven."

Matthew 18:19

PRAYER NUGGETS

DATE _____
S M T W T F S

PRAISE & WORSHIP SONGS

PRAYER SCRIPTURES

WORD OF KNOWLEDGE

MEMORY VERSE

PRAYER REQUESTS
- [ ]
- [ ]
- [ ]

PRAYER TESTIMONY

WISDOM NUGGETS

PRAYER ACTIONS
- [ ]
- [ ]
- [ ]

MY PASSION FOR PRAYER TODAY
☆ ☆ ☆ ☆ ☆

NOTES

"But now be courageous, Zerubbabel,' declares the LORD, 'be courageous also, Joshua the son of Jehozadak, the high priest, and be courageous, all you people of the land,' declares the LORD, 'and work; for I am with you,' declares the LORD of hosts."

HAGGAI 2:4

PRAYER NUGGETS

DATE _____
S M T W T F S

PRAISE & WORSHIP SONGS

PRAYER SCRIPTURES

WORD OF KNOWLEDGE

MEMORY VERSE

PRAYER REQUESTS
- [ ]
- [ ]
- [ ]

PRAYER TESTIMONY

WISDOM NUGGETS

PRAYER ACTIONS
- [ ]
- [ ]
- [ ]

MY PASSION FOR PRAYER TODAY
☆ ☆ ☆ ☆ ☆

NOTES

"Then David said to his son Solomon, "Be strong and courageous, and take action; do not fear nor be dismayed, for the LORD God, my God, is with you. He will not fail you nor abandon you [but will guide you in the construction] until you have finished all the work for the service of the house of the LORD"

1 CHRONICLES 28:20

PRAYER NUGGETS

DATE _____
S M T W T F S

PRAISE & WORSHIP SONGS

WORD OF KNOWLEDGE

PRAYER SCRIPTURES

MEMORY VERSE

PRAYER REQUESTS
- ☐
- ☐
- ☐

WISDOM NUGGETS

PRAYER TESTIMONY

PRAYER ACTIONS
- ☐
- ☐
- ☐

MY PASSION FOR PRAYER TODAY
☆ ☆ ☆ ☆ ☆

NOTES

"Let everything you do be done in love [motivated and inspired by God's love for us]."

1 Corinthians 16:14

ABOUT THE AUTHOR

Caroline Bimbo Afolalu is a Christian, devoted to God and prayers. Since childhood, she has been a Christian but officially gave her life to the Lord Jesus Christ in the summer of 1986 at a Christian crusade in Akure, Nigeria, West Africa before migrating to the United Kingdom in 1992.

Caroline works as a company director with a demonstrated history of working in the food production industry since 2001. She is the founder and director of Beautiful Foods Ltd the owner of Tabitha's brand of Chin Chin, a West African Nigerian Snack operating in London UK.

Caroline is married to Tunde Afolalu since September 1992, they have, three wonderful and successful children - Adebisi, Pelumi, and Grace Ife Afolalu.

Caroline believes in marketplace ministry. She runs a daily prayer and teaching YouTube channel (prayer nuggets) and Tabitha's Charity with a focus on village women in Nigerian villages, alongside running her food manufacturing business in the United Kingdom.

Caroline would like to simply be known as Mrs Caroline Bimbo Afolalu the great! Achieving greatness in the simplest ways as a daughter, wife, mother, businessperson, and woman of God.

OTHER BOOKS FROM THE AUTHOR

How to Start a Business - A Guide to Starting and Growing a Food Business

Beautiful Foods - The Art of African Catering

The Names of God – How to pray with God's names

How to Do Life – Wisdom Nuggets from Proverbs

Upcoming Books

The Promised Life - Wisdom Nuggets from Joshua

CONTACT DETAILS

Websites

Work
www.beautifulfoods.co.uk
www.tabithaschinchin.com

Charity
www.prayernuggets.com

WORKS CITED

The Holy Bible

RECOMMENDED RESOURCES

The Holy Bible

"For God so [greatly] loved *and* dearly prized the world, that He [even] gave His [One and] only begotten Son, so that whoever believes *and* trusts in Him [as Saviour] shall not perish, but have eternal life"

JOHN 3:16

www.ingramcontent.com/pod-product-compliance
Lightning Source LLC
Chambersburg PA
CBHW051945290426
44110CB00015B/2111